D0118645

EXTREME ENVIRONMENTAL THREATS™

THE RISING SEAS

Shorelines Under Threat

Ellen Foxxe

The Rosen Publishing Group, Inc., New York

To my niece and nephew, Laura and Matthew Freedman, with love.

Published in 2007 by The Rosen Publishing Group, Inc.
29 East 21st Street, New York, NY 10010

First Edition

Library of Congress Cataloging-in-Publication Data

Foxxe, Ellen.
The rising seas: shorelines under threat/by Ellen Foxxe.—1st ed.
        p. cm.—(Extreme environmental threats)
Includes bibliographical references (p.   ) and index.
ISBN 1-4042-0742-2 (library binding)
1. Sea level—Juvenile literature. 2. Coast changes—Juvenile literature.
3. Climatic changes—Juvenile literature. I. Title. II. Series.
GC89.F69 2006
551.45'8—dc22

                                                        2006000053

Manufactured in the United States of America

On the cover: People walk through a flooded street in Dhaka, Bangladesh. Rising seas and increased floods are affecting the lives of people worldwide. They have had the greatest impact on poor and developing countries. **Title page:** A boy carries his goat through floodwaters near Dhaka, Bangladesh. In August 2002, annual monsoon flooding left 157 dead and nearly 7 million people displaced from their homes.

Contents

INTRODUCTION

When land-based ice melts, such as the ice on the continent of Antarctica, it adds to the sea's volume.

Sea levels are not only rising, they are doing so at a much faster rate than in previous centuries. There is a great deal of scientific data that links this rise to human activities during the past 200 years. The impact of actions such as the burning of fossil fuels and the use of nitrogen-based fertilizer to grow food has become greater and greater throughout the twentieth and twenty-first centuries.

The continuing rise in sea levels could have disastrous effects on land and people around the world. Scientists

estimate that during the past century the height of the sea has risen 0.4 to 1 inch (1 to 2.5 centimeters) per year. Computer models indicate that sea levels will rise at two to five times that rate during the twenty-first century. The Arctic Climate Impact Assessment, an international research project that released its results in 2004, calculates that temperatures in western Canada, Alaska, and eastern Russia have risen as much as four to seven degrees Fahrenheit (two to four degrees Celsius) in the last fifty years. The report also estimates that temperatures are likely to increase another 7° to 13°F (4° to 7°C) during the next century. The continuation in temperature increases likely means ongoing glacier and ice sheet melting.

Even if only 10 percent of Antarctic ice melts, the level of the seas could rise by twelve to thirty feet (four to nine meters). If half the Arctic ice sheets melt by the end of the twenty-first century, as the Arctic Climate Impact Assessment says is likely, sea levels could rise by 23 feet (7 m). This change in sea level will have great effects on the geographical shape of the world and people's lives.

Understanding what is causing the rise of sea levels is the first step in reducing the factors that create such problems. Action must be taken to diminish rising sea levels' effects on coastal communities. In addition, approaches that will reduce or eliminate the causes of rising seas must be developed.

This book examines rising sea levels and how human populations are contributing to this rise. It also discusses current scientific research and approaches for coping with the changes that increasing sea levels may bring.

An aerial photograph taken on August 26, 2005, shows South Miami-Dade County in Florida after the area was struck by Hurricane Katrina.

Earth's mountain and polar glaciers continue to melt, man-made pollution continues to fuel the greenhouse effect, and global warming continues to increase. Temperatures in the upper layers of the ocean rise, and tall crests of wind-driven seawater crash along the coast more often.

SWEEPING AWAY NEW YORK CITY?

Scientists are studying what could occur as a result of these changes. Could massive flooding swallow up

Pedestrians walk under huge waves that crashed over the seawall in Torquay, which is in southwest England, on October 27, 2004. Gale-force winds drove an exceptionally high tide over the seawall, flooding dozens of homes. It was the worst flooding in the area in thirty years.

thousands of miles of shoreline surrounding the New York City area, leveling buildings and leaving millions injured, dead, or homeless? A report from the U.S. National Aeronautics and Space Administration (NASA) Goddard Institute for Space Studies at Columbia University in New York City suggests that such a scenario is possible. According to Vivien Gornitz's 2000 report "Rising Seas: A View from New York City," as sea level rises, floodwaters from storms could swamp parts of lower Manhattan and the boroughs of Queens and Staten Island. Rail and subway transportation systems would come to a stop, and local airports, which are only three feet above current sea level, would be forced to close.

Given the current rate at which the sea level is rising, by the end of this century, parts of lower Manhattan, Queens, Coney Island, and other New York City areas could be covered by floodwaters on a regular basis. This could occur anywhere from once every fifty years to as frequently as once every four years.

DESTRUCTION OF THE GULF COAST

The idea that a hurricane could destroy entire cities once might have seemed like science fiction. However, in August 2005, Hurricane Katrina smashed into the southern United States around the Gulf of Mexico. And what seemed like a scene from a disaster movie became a devastating reality.

Hurricanes are categorized on a scale of intensity from 1 to 5, with 5 being the most intense. Hurricane Katrina made landfall as a category 4 hurricane. According to statistics released at a 2005 press conference by Federal Emergency Management Agency (FEMA), U.S. Army Corps of Engineers, Coast Guard, and Red Cross officials, Hurricane Katrina cut a path of destruction across 90,000 square miles (233,000 square kilometers)—an area larger than Great Britain. Katrina leveled entire towns and cities in Mississippi, Alabama, and Louisiana.

In August 2005, Hurricane Katrina led to one of the most devastating floods in U.S. history. This photo shows New Orleans, Louisiana, the day after the hurricane. Highway ramps were used to launch boats into the flooded streets. The boat rescuers helped people who had become trapped in their homes, some of which were flooded to roof level.

It damaged levees in New Orleans so extensively that almost the entire city flooded. Water poured over the Industrial Canal on the east side of the city. On the opposite side of the city, water broke through the 17th Street levee, which carried water between the Mississippi River and Lake Pontchartrain. Many buildings were crushed by the sheer force of the water pouring in, and for weeks afterward, many more sat in up to 20 feet (6 m) of water. More than a thousand people lost their lives, and hundreds of thousands were evacuated and/or left homeless. In the wake of Hurricane Katrina, almost a million people applied to the federal government for assistance. Experts estimate that it will take many years and billions of dollars for the Gulf Coast to recover from Katrina's fury.

DROWNING FLORIDA

Florida is likely to be another state that will fall victim to rising seas. The Florida Keys, a group of islands off the southern coast of Florida, may disappear completely. Measurements taken by the U.S. Environmental Protection Agency (EPA) at Key West, a major resort island, show that the sea level there has increased about 1 foot (0.3 m) since 1846. It is increasing at the rate of 15 inches (4 cm) every hundred years, which is a great deal for an area where the height of land is, at most, only 3 feet (1 m) above sea level. If water rose 1 foot (0.3 m) over the next century, it would cover some of the islands completely. A rise in sea level would also have negative effects on southern Florida's ecosystem (the area's plants and animals), affecting coral reefs, mangrove trees, and sea grass.

DEATH OF THE MANGROVES

The mangrove tree groves in southern Florida perform a variety of important functions. They anchor sediments

Mangroves, a type of tropical ever-green tree, have stilt-like roots and stems. They form dense thickets along coastlines, providing invaluable protection for the plants and animals that live there.

(deposits of minerals and other solid material) and help protect the shoreline from being washed away; filter out pollution; and provide food and homes for nearly 500 species of fish, birds, amphibians, reptiles, and mammals. However, the rising seas threaten these important mangrove communities. Sea level is projected to rise by 1 foot (0.3 m) during the next century, but some researchers believe that 4 to 5 inches (10 to 13 cm) is all the mangroves can survive.

BATTERING THE COAST OF CANADA

In Canada, along the coast of the Bay of Fundy, which is an inlet of ocean between New Brunswick and Nova Scotia, the sea level has risen 14 inches (35 cm) over the past century. Some experts predict that the sea could rise from 20 to 27 inches (51 to 68 cm) in the next

Coasts in Danger

According to the EPA, areas that are especially in danger from rising seas include the coastal areas of New York (New York City and Long Island), Massachusetts (Cape Cod and Boston), Maine, Delaware Bay, New Jersey, Chesapeake Bay and Maryland, North Carolina, South Carolina, Georgia, Florida (especially southern Florida), and the Gulf Coast areas of Louisiana, Mississippi, and Alabama. The Atlantic coast of Canada is also a danger zone. An EPA report, "Greenhouse Effect and Sea Level Rise: The Cost of Holding Back the Sea," states that "if no measures are taken to hold back the sea, a one meter rise [3.28 feet] in sea level would inundate 14,000 square miles [36,260 sq km], with wet and dry land each accounting for about half the loss." In addition to direct destruction caused by floodwaters and sea surges, such flooding could have other, longer-lasting effects. The seawater would contaminate the affected areas' water tables with salt. This would reduce the amount of available water suitable for drinking and crop irrigation.

Aerial view of Martha's Vineyard   Computer-enhanced view

The photo at left shows Martha's Vineyard, an island off the coast of Massachusetts, as it exists today. The photo at right shows how Martha's Vineyard will look if sea levels were to rise by 3 feet (1 m).

hundred years. In addition, global warming is increasing the ocean's temperature around the Atlantic coast of Canada. In the past, most tropical storms weakened when they reached the cold water around Canada. (The cold water protects the coast from the severe hurricanes that strike in warmer areas such as Florida.) As the water around Canada increases in temperature, however, more of these storms may survive and hammer the coast.

In 1869, a huge storm called the Great Saxby Gale struck the area around the Bay of Fundy. Entire coastal communities were flooded as the tide rose nearly 6.5 feet (2 m) in some places. Buildings were swept away, hundreds of boats were beached or sunk by high winds, and dozens of people and farm animals drowned.

Given the current combination of rising seas and increasing global warming, such storms may again hit Canada and do so more frequently in the next century. Because such storms have been rare, people and communities are not prepared to face them. At the same time, the population has grown and the number of buildings in coastal areas has increased. As a result, damage from such future storms could be much worse than it was 150 years ago.

CAUSES OF RISING SEAS

As the ice at the base of glaciers and ice shelves melt, pieces break off, or calve, and slide into the sea. This photo shows ice in the Ross Sea near Antarctica.

The global rise in sea level comes from several sources. There is no doubt that glaciers and ice in the Arctic and Antarctic are melting at a more rapid pace than in the past. Sea levels are also increasing because of its heating up in many places.

DRIPPING GLACIERS

One of the major causes of rising seas is the melting of glaciers, large sheets of ice that move slowly across land.

Glaciers exist on every continent except Australia. There are several different types of glaciers. Some of these glaciers are located in the mountains. Glaciers can also spread from mountainous regions to cover flat land. Huge ice sheets can cover all terrain for miles around. Much of this ice is found in the Arctic and Antarctic. Glaciers collect and store rain and snow as ice. People who live near glaciers use melted glacial ice for drinking water and to irrigate farmland. This water also provides hydroelectric power. Hydroelectric power uses rushing water to rotate the blades of a wheel connected to a machine called a generator that, in turn, produces electricity.

There is evidence that the size of glaciers around the world is shrinking. For example, in 1910 the Danish Geodetic Survey measured the Ok ice cap in western Iceland. Today, bare ground can be seen in parts of the ice cap that were covered with a 100-foot-thick (30 m) sheet of ice less than a hundred years ago. Glaciologists, scientists who study glaciers, have discovered that hundreds of glaciers have become smaller during the last century. They estimate that 15 percent of the total amount of glacier ice has melted. Since 1850, the glaciers in the high, icy Alps have shrunk 50 percent.

Scientists all over the world are noticing the same thing. In the 1990s, the Soviet Geophysical Committee discovered that 85 percent of Asia's 408 glaciers had shrunk over the preceding forty years. Shrinking glaciers have also been recorded in the Canadian Rockies, New Zealand, Scandinavia, Kenya, and Kazakhstan. The United Nations Intergovernmental Panel on Climate Change studies the effects of global warming. The panel has agreed that glaciers in the Alps are melting ten times faster now than they did at the end of the last ice age, which occurred between 10,000 and 20,000 years ago. The rate at which the massive Greenland Ice Sheet is melting is 16 percent greater now than it was twenty years ago.

A stream of meltwater, above, cascades off the vast Arctic ice sheet that covers much of Greenland. Arctic sea ice has decreased significantly in the last half-century.

GLACIERS AND SEA LEVEL

As much as 40 percent of the increase in sea level in the 1990s may be the result of glacial melting. Many glaciers are located in areas where temperatures are very close to 32°F (0°C), the temperature at which ice remains frozen. This is true, for example, in Peru's Andes mountains and in the mountains of other non-Arctic countries. In these areas, a small temperature increase can lead to melting ice.

Glaciers provide water for a variety of uses, such as drinking, irrigation, and electric power. Shrinking glaciers have already produced water shortages in many areas, including communities in the Alps; the Andes; and the Cascade Range, which provides water for Washington State. Even more serious is the fact that the melting of the glaciers has contributed to a sea level rise of 5 inches (13 cm) since 1940.

One recent discovery by scientists indicates that Alaskan glaciers may be melting and producing more meltwater than previously thought. Alaska has more than 29,000 square miles (75,000 sq km) of glacial ice. Alaska contains the biggest glaciers found outside the North Pole and South Pole. Frequently, data from Alaskan glaciers has not been included in computer models that focus on Antarctic and European glacial melting. Therefore, the potential rise in sea level from glacial melting may be even greater than previously thought.

THE ARCTIC ICE CAP

The Arctic's summer ice sheet is 40 percent thinner now than it was fifty years ago, and its surface is only

85 percent of its former size. Since Arctic temperatures are the warmest they have been in 400 years, the ice sheet is likely to keep on thinning. In 2004, the results of the Arctic Climate Impact Assessment, a four-year study carried out by an international team of more than 300 scientists, was released. According to the study, temperatures in Arctic regions have increased during the past fifty years and are likely to continue rising. The study predicts that as much as half the Arctic ice sheet, including a large section of the Greenland Ice Sheet, is likely to melt by the end of the twenty-first century. This would cause a significant increase in sea level.

ANTARCTIC GLACIERS

Antarctica is covered with glaciers. Scientists have categorized these sheets as the East Antarctica Ice Sheet and the West Antarctica Ice Sheet. The West Antarctica Ice Sheet is more than 3,280 feet (1 km) thick and flows into the Ross Sea, filling the area with floating ice. It is of interest to ecologists (scientists who study the environment) because its melting was one of the factors that led to past ice ages. An ice age is an extended period of time when there is a decrease in the average global temperature. Initially, warmer temperatures lead to the melting of land-based ice sheets. However, as the ice melts, this cold water slows the ocean currents that bring warm water to continental coasts. Thus, the climate becomes colder.

An ice shelf is a thick mass of ice that extends from coastal land and floats into the sea. Ice shelves are fed by glacial flow, which increases the amount of ice. In 1995, the Larsen A ice shelf in the Antarctic, which was about 600 square miles (1,600 sq km), shattered. In 1998, a 77-square-mile (199 sq km) sheet of ice broke off the Antarctic's Larsen B Ice Shelf. In 2002, the Larsen B Ice Shelf broke off completely. It poured 720 billion tons (653 billion metric tons) of ice into the sea. According to the National Snow and Ice Data Center (NSIDC), scientists who conducted studies of ice cores say this may have been the first time in 12,000 years that the ice collapsed. These scientists have stated that a possible reason for the breaking up of ice shelves may be summer temperatures. If the temperatures get warm enough, the meltwater may form ponds on the ice. The meltwater can then leak into small cracks in the shelf's surface. If there is enough water and the cracks are deep enough, the water may cause the cracks to expand and split off ice.

The Thwaites Glacier in West Antarctica also concerns scientists. In 1999, ice broke off the glacier and formed two icebergs. The U.S. National Oceanic and Atmospheric Administration (NOAA) reported one of these icebergs as being one and a half times the size

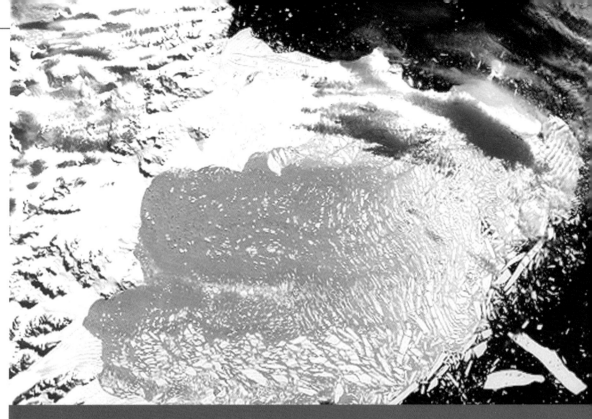

This photo, taken on March 7, 2002, by a NASA satellite, shows the Larsen B ice shelf that shattered and separated from the eastern side of the Antarctic Peninsula. The shelf had existed since the last ice age 12,000 years ago, but collapsed in 2002, during one of the warmest Antarctic summers on record. The destroyed area was 1,040 square miles (2,694 sq km) and released 720 billion tons (nearly 655 billion metric tons) of ice.

of the state of Delaware. Some scientists fear that rapid melting of the Thwaites Glacier could cause sea levels to rise by up to 16.5 feet (5 m).

If these ice sheets slide into the sea, sea level around the world would rise by as much as 300 feet (91 m). Such a rise would engulf coastal areas worldwide, washing away entire towns and drowning island communities such as those on the Marshall Islands in the Pacific Ocean.

Researchers predict that the Marshall Islands, above, could lose 80 percent of their land if sea level rises 20 inches (0.5 m). Many islands in the South Pacific and the Indian Ocean, such as those in French Polynesia and the Maldives, could disappear completely if levels continue to rise.

Satellite data from the Jet Propulsion Laboratory (JPL) in Pasadena, California, raises questions as to whether the West Antarctica Ice Sheet is actually melting. According to satellite data analyzed by Ian Joughin of JPL, the rate of movement of some of the West Antarctic Ice Sheet, such as the Whillans Ice Stream, may be slowing. Movement in other parts of the sheet, such as the Pine Island Ice Stream, is increasing, however, so what the end result will be is unclear. It is important that scientists learn more about what is happening in this area of Antarctica because a significant increase or decrease in ice has important implications. For instance, a major increase in cold water entering the ocean from melting glaciers will alter ocean currents responsible for maintaining moderate temperatures around the world.

THERMAL EXPANSION

Prior to the 1980s, scientists thought that melting Antarctic glaciers were the major cause of rising sea levels. Today, however, most scientists think that thermal expansion is the biggest reason for the rising seas. What is thermal expansion? It is a process in which something expands to take up more space as it heats up. Heat causes things to expand, and cold causes them to contract.

Water, like everything else on Earth, is made up of molecules. Molecules are clusters of atoms, the basic particles that make up matter. Water molecules are too small to see with the naked eye, but they are constantly in motion. The colder water gets, the less the molecules move and the more they clump together. When water gets cold enough, it becomes ice. The reverse is also true. The warmer water gets, the more the molecules move apart and the more space the water takes up. This is what is happening as a result of global warming. The sea gets warmer and expands, but because land surrounds it, the sea cannot spread out forever. Instead, it starts to get higher, much like the water level in a glass when it is refilled.

Many scientists who have studied satellite data to learn how much the Antarctic ice sheets are melting now feel that thermal expansion of warming seawater

How Permanent Is Permafrost?

Permafrost is ground that stays continuously frozen for two or more years. Some permafrost is found on land. However, it can also occur beneath the continental shelves in the Arctic. The frozen ground's thickness ranges from 3.28 to 3,280 feet (1 to 1,000 m). The thaw of permafrost can lead to the collapse of man-made structures that were built on it. It can also cause landslides. One effect of global warming is that in some regions such as Alaska, permafrost is melting. When the permafrost melts, it changes an area's ecosystem. For instance, areas of

Trees in Fairbanks, Alaska, lean at dangerous angles as a result of the once-solid permafrost melting beneath the trees. Temperatures in Northern Alaska have increased over the past forty years because of global warming. Scientists predict that in the next sixty years, permafrost across Alaska will disappear. This could cause untold damage to roads, homes, pipelines, and other structures.

Arctic tundra (treeless plains with frozen soil) will be able to support forest. If changes in plant life occur, animals that live on the tundra, such as moose and caribou, will likely be affected. Some scientists predict that in the next fifty years temperatures in the Arctic will increase by as much as 9°F (5°C). The effects of this climatic change have yet to be understood. For example, since thawed ground emits greenhouse gases such as carbon dioxide (CO_2) and methane (CH_4), and frozen soil doesn't, will a widespread thawing of permafrost result in further global warming?

Alaska isn't the only place where permafrost is in danger. Scientists from Tomsk State University in Siberia, Russia, and Oxford University in the United Kingdom are worried that permafrost covering 386,000 square miles (1,000,000 sq km) in western Siberia is melting. They fear that if this permafrost melts, it could release vast amounts of greenhouse gases into the atmosphere.

and the melting of mountain glaciers, not Antarctic glaciers, are the largest contributors to rising seas.

There is little doubt that melting ice and thermal expansion are contributing to an increase in sea levels. But what is the cause of this meltdown?

Many of the pollutants that industrial smoke-stacks expel into the atmosphere contain greenhouse gas molecules that will take decades, or longer, to disperse into space.

Many human activities, such as burning fossil fuels, have led to a rise in global warming. Global warming is an increase in the average temperature of the atmosphere, and it results from an accumulation of certain gases. Atoms of carbon (C), oxygen (O), hydrogen (H), and nitrogen (N) combine to form gas molecules. The most damaging of these gases are carbon dioxide (CO_2), methane (CH_4), and nitrous oxide (N_2O). The gases have always existed in the atmosphere in tiny amounts. But the quantity has soared dramatically in the past 200 years.

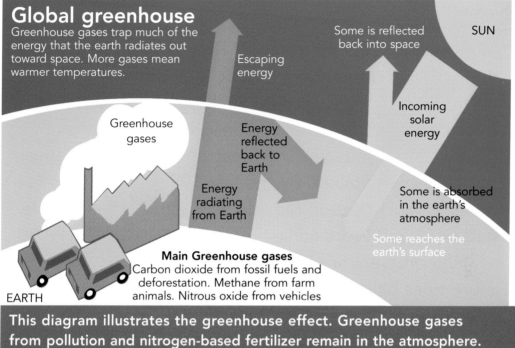

Global greenhouse

Greenhouse gases trap much of the energy that the earth radiates out toward space. More gases mean warmer temperatures.

Escaping energy

Some is reflected back into space

SUN

Incoming solar energy

Greenhouse gases

Energy reflected back to Earth

Energy radiating from Earth

Some is absorbed in the earth's atmosphere

Some reaches the earth's surface

EARTH

Main Greenhouse gases
Carbon dioxide from fossil fuels and deforestation. Methane from farm animals. Nitrous oxide from vehicles

This diagram illustrates the greenhouse effect. Greenhouse gases from pollution and nitrogen-based fertilizer remain in the atmosphere. Molecules of these gases reflect sunlight back to the earth, causing temperatures to rise. Carbon dioxide accounts for over 90 percent of greenhouse gases. Methane, nitrous oxide, and other greenhouse gases also contribute to global warming.

These gases come from human activities such as burning fossil fuels (oil, gas, or coal) to run cars, manufacturing goods, and heating an ever-growing number of homes and commercial buildings.

THE GREENHOUSE EFFECT

The molecules of most of the components in the air we breathe, such as oxygen and nitrogen, are transparent to sunlight. That is, light passes right through them. The molecules that make up the greenhouse gases, however, do not allow sunlight through. They absorb, or capture, the light and then reflect it back to Earth, where it heats up the planet. This is known as the greenhouse effect because these gases reflect sunlight like the panes of glass in a greenhouse. The most significant greenhouse gas is carbon dioxide. By the late 1990s, more than five times as much carbon dioxide was in the air than there had been 250 years earlier.

The problem has been made worse as more and more trees have been cut down to grow crops and put up buildings. Trees use carbon dioxide, along with sunlight and water, as part of photosynthesis—the process by which plants make food for themselves. The fewer trees there are, the more carbon dioxide there is in the atmosphere. Thus, simultaneously more carbon dioxide is being produced (by burning fossil fuels) and the natural resources that process it are being reduced. This combination could very well spell trouble for Earth and its population in the years ahead.

During the past 400,000 years, temperatures have changed in relation to increases and decreases in the atmosphere's concentration of greenhouse gases. During the last 1,500 years, the sea level rose about 4 inches (10 cm) per century. The current rate of rise, however, is twice that. In addition, the twentieth century was the

This aerial view of the Amazon rain forest shows an area where hundreds of acres of forest have recently been cut down for lumber, and to make space for farming and raising cattle. The Brazilian government has announced that during the twelve months ending in August 2004, 10,089 square miles (26,130 sq km) of the Amazon Basin were destroyed.

warmest century in 1,000 years. Many scientists think that pollution from greenhouse gases is one of the major causes of this increase in temperature.

TURNING UP THE THERMOSTAT

One of the effects of global warming is the melting of polar ice caps and glaciers. The UN Intergovernmental Panel on Climate Change has stated that the shrinking of

Back to the Future?

The last time that the glaciers melted was 130,000 years ago. Scientists have examined island coral at Key West, Florida, and the Seychelles (in the western Indian Ocean), among other islands. They have found corals in geological formations dating from that period that are about 10 to 20 feet (3 to 6 m) higher than those underwater today. From this, they can tell that the sea was 10 to 20 feet (3 to 6 m) higher then than it is today.

At that time, the average temperature was 5.4° to 9°F (3° to 5°C) higher than it is today. Scientists have figured this out based on the fossil remains of plants and animals found there and their knowledge of the temperatures in which these organisms are able to survive. They estimate that, as a result of global warming, the temperature will again increase by that amount by the end of the twenty-first century.

Increases in sea temperature are killing coral reefs around the Seychelles islands and the unique species of animals and fish that live in them.

the glaciers is "among the clearest and best evidence" of changes in the climate during the last hundred years. The way that humans are changing the climate and sea levels can have serious consequences for all of us. Therefore, it is important for scientists to monitor the changes that are taking place.

4 UNLOCKING THE SECRETS OF THE SEAS

A color-enhanced satellite image of the Byrd Glacier on the coast of Antarctica.

Scientists use a variety of tools to study the seas in an effort to understand the changes that are taking place. Some of these are tools that aid scientists with direct on-site observation. Others are automated and can see and record things that people cannot because these things are too small to see or too remote to access without great difficulty. Many techniques used to monitor changes in the climate and the sea have become possible only with the technological advances of the twentieth and twenty-first centuries.

MODELING THE SEAS

Computer models are one approach that scientists use to understand the effects of rising seas. Scientists know that various aspects of climate such as temperature, precipitation, wind, and humidity affect one another. For example, as temperatures rise in response to the output of greenhouse gases, they will cause changes in rain, wind, and ice melt. Scientists have developed complicated mathematical formulas that can be used to predict what will happen to climatic conditions in response to changes in various factors. In a computer model, scientists feed data about different aspects of climate into a computer, along with mathematical formulas.

Computer models can be used to predict the likelihood of storms, flooding, and other effects of rising seas on coastal cities. They can also predict the probable effects of emitting high concentrations of greenhouse gases into the atmosphere.

MATHEMATICAL MODELS

Sometimes an area has no historical data, but scientists need to estimate the effects that rising seas will have on it. In this case, scientists sometimes use mathematical formulas. For example, a formula called the Brunn rule estimates coastal erosion in response to sea level. This rule states that the shoreline keeps its shape but moves forward and back as the level of the sea changes. Scientists can then insert different sea levels into the formula to predict how far the shoreline will retreat.

Such mathematical predictions must be applied carefully, however, because the rate at which coastline recedes may vary. This type of calculation works well when the coastal land is sand or dirt, but it may not be accurate when the shoreline is composed of rock, which is less likely to be washed away.

AIRBORNE MEASUREMENT

Another approach that scientists take relies on direct observation. Measurements of a variety of factors related to sea level, coastal erosion, and glacial melting are taken and studied over a long period of time. Based on what has happened in the past, scientists can use this data to estimate what is likely to occur in the future. In this type of analysis, it is important to take all possible relevant factors into account. Just because something has been occurring doesn't mean that it will continue to occur, or occur at the same rate in the future.

Although direct observation is the oldest scientific method, a few new twists have been added as technology has advanced. Scientists have been using a

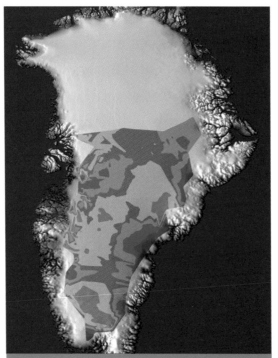

This image, showing loss of ice per year on Greenland, was produced by comparing laser altimetry data taken in 1993–1994 to 1998–1999. Areas of ice loss range from –2 cm *(light blue)* to –60 cm *(dark blue)*. In other areas, ice has increased from 2 cm *(light yellow)* to 60 cm *(orange)*.

method called airborne laser altimetry, for example, to observe glaciers. This process, also called airborne laser scanning, uses a laser located on an aircraft. Short flashes from the laser are bounced off the surface of an object on Earth. It then measures the length of time it takes for the light to be reflected back to the instrument. Based on the time measurement, the instrument can then calculate the distance of the object. A computer processes the data from a series of measurements and can produce a type of map of the surface measured. Scientists are able to collect as much data in a single day using airborne laser altimetry as a survey team on the ground could collect in several weeks.

In one study, for example, a group of scientists used this technology to learn how the size of sixty-seven glaciers in Alaska and nearby Canada has shrunk from the mid-1950s to the early twenty-first century. They have shown that recent melting of Alaskan glaciers is almost twice as great as that previously thought to come from the entire Greenland Ice Sheet (one of the largest Arctic ice sheets). This means that the Alaskan glaciers are the biggest contributor of glacial meltwater to the rising seas.

Submarine Observation

Direct observation sometimes involves going down rather than up. The depth of sea ice, for example, cannot be observed from above. Scientists have used submarines to go below the surface of Arctic ice floes. They have found that the ice currently extends 4.3 feet (1.3 m) less beneath the surface of sea ice than it did thirty to forty years ago. The melting of sea ice does not increase the volume of water in the sea because the meltwater merely replaces the space occupied by the ice. The rate at which it melts, however, provides scientists with valuable information about increasing temperatures and their effects on Arctic ice in general.

A U.S. Navy submarine is shown surfacing through Arctic ice. Submarines use methods such as sonar (sound wave) measurements to collect data about ice.

SATELLITE OBSERVATION

This satellite image shows icebergs breaking out of sea ice in the Southern Ocean surrounding the Antarctic Peninsula. Warmer temperatures have caused ice on the tip of the peninsula to melt, leaving a patch of bare ground.

Satellite observation is one of the handiest tools for scientific observation of natural forces such as glacial melting. Instruments on satellites can observe large areas of Earth's surface that are too big to be observed from the ground, such as glaciers that stretch for hundreds or thousands of miles.

Since the 1970s, a type of satellite-based technology called passive microwave data has been used to provide images of ice cover in polar oceans. Microwaves are short waves of energy with electric and magnetic properties. All objects give off microwave energy. This energy is not visible to the naked eye, but it can be picked up and recorded by electronic devices such as those on satellites. Microwave energy penetrates clouds and fog and therefore allows scientists to monitor features on Earth that cannot be seen because of cloud cover. Passive microwave imaging devices that have been placed on satellites include the Scanning Multichannel Microwave Radiometer, launched by NASA in 1978, and the Special Sensor Microwave Imager, which the U.S. Defense Meteorological Satellite Program launched in 1987.

Passive microwave technology allows scientists to monitor changes in ice edges and the depth and types of ice found in polar regions. By using this technology, scientists have discovered that Arctic ice cover decreased by 3 percent over the last decade of the twentieth century. The amount of sea ice (free-floating ice in the Arctic sea) decreased to record lows for three years running, from 2002 to 2004. This has led scientists at the National Snow and Ice Data Center (NSIDC) to conclude that the amount of polar sea ice is declining at the rate of 7.7 percent per decade.

TRACKING SNOW COVER

Satellite-based sensors are also used to track the amount of snow cover that exists in various locations. Snow cover is the amount of snow that builds up on the ground in a specific location, as opposed to the amount of snow that falls from the sky, some of which may melt. Snow cover is an important factor in the climate because snow reflects a lot of light. It reflects 80 to 90 percent of

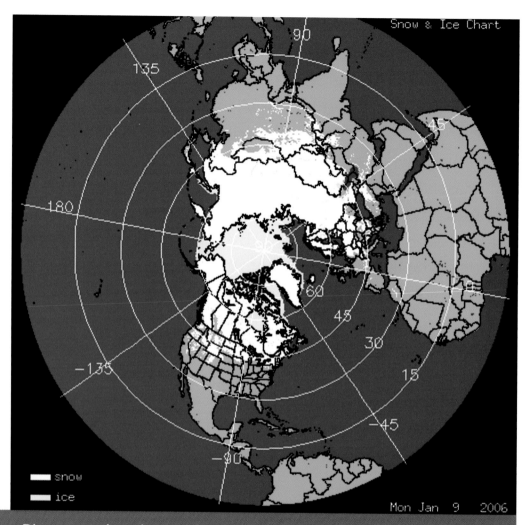

Diagrams such as the one above, which charts snow and ice in the Northern Hemisphere, allow scientists to keep track of changes in ice cover. Experts collect data about land, sea, sea ice, and snow using a wide variety of satellites that provide imaging data and microwave measurements.

the energy that comes from the sun back into space. Ground not covered by snow absorbs 80 to 90 percent of the heat from the sun. For forty years, scientists in industrialized nations around the world such as Europe and the United States have used satellite-based sensors to track the worldwide amount of snow cover. The National Oceanic and Atmospheric Administration produces weekly maps of the snow in the Northern Hemisphere.

Data indicates that for the past twenty-four years, summer snow cover in the Northern Hemisphere has been decreasing by 3 to 5 percent per decade. The actual amount of snow cover and rain that has occurred during this period has remained steady. It therefore appears that the decrease in snow is the result of higher temperatures. Less snow cover means that the exposed ground absorbs more heat. This heating up of the soil could extend the growing season in some cold regions, such as Scandinavia, but could also lead to drought conditions in other areas such as eastern Africa.

THE FUTURE LANDSCAPE

The Seine River in Paris, seen here after a storm submerged roads that cross it.

Scientists predict that sometime in the twenty-first century the level of carbon dioxide in the atmosphere will be double what it was in preindustrial times. This greenhouse gas increase is likely to cause significant climatic changes. The variations in climate will mean that some areas that are now forests or areas used for farming will become unsuitable for these purposes. Meanwhile, other areas that were previously unable to support forests or farmable land will become more suitable. These transformations will affect the animals that live in these environments. Changes in climate

Bangladeshi children cross a makeshift bridge during floods in July 2002. Overflowing rivers broke through mud embankments and poured into a third of Bangladesh's villages. Secondary effects such as flood-related disease add to the damage inflicted by these enormous amounts of water, and will cause greater problems if floods occur more frequently.

will also affect people's ability to grow food and have drinkable water. Floods, droughts, and coastal storms are likely to become more frequent and will also affect people's health.

One effect of the ice melting in Arctic and Antarctic regions is an increase in the number of icebergs in the sea. The melting of the permafrost in these regions is also likely to lead to the release of greenhouse gases such as carbon dioxide and methane. This could further increase global warming.

Rising seas and more frequent severe storms will have a direct effect on people's health. Powerful storms and floods will likely lead to an increased number of drowning deaths and disaster-related injuries. After such disasters, survivors will be more likely to catch diseases because they will be exposed to germs and chemicals in floodwater. In addition, food, clean water, electricity, and health care may not be adequate or available. Millions of people could be left homeless and starving. Even without storm damage, diseases such as cholera (an intestinal disease), giardiasis (an intestinal parasite), malaria (a disease caused by a parasite spread by mosquitoes), dengue fever (a virus spread by mosquitoes), and salmonellosis (an intestinal disease) are likely to spread in response to higher temperatures and more frequent flooding.

A rise in average temperature of a few degrees may not seem like much, but an increase of only 3.5°F (2°C) would mean that the earth would experience temperatures that have not been experienced for 125,000 years. An increase of 5.5°F (3°C) would increase temperatures to the level of two million years ago.

STORMS OVER EUROPE

The effects of increased storms and rising seas could be intensified as a result of other naturally occurring conditions. The coast of the United Kingdom and the area of Germany fed by the Rhine River both already have problems with seawater washing onto land. A disaster in the Netherlands in 1953 provides an example of what can happen when high seas combine with other conditions. In this case, on January 31, 1953, a weather depression (an area where the atmospheric pressure is lower than that of the surrounding air) approached the Netherlands. It was high tide, and heavy rain had made the sea rise even higher, producing flooding. The low pressure at the center of the depression caused the level of the sea to rise 1.6 feet (0.5 m), and the increased winds created waves almost 20 feet (6 m) high. The sea was so high that it poured over the sea walls that were supposed to hold it back, covering one-sixth of the Netherlands with water. As a result, 1,835 people were killed. Although in this case the sea level was high because it was high tide, the effect would be the same if seas were high for other reasons. If higher sea levels exist in the future, this deadly combination of high seas with naturally occurring events such as weather depressions could become more common.

FLOODING

Flooding could affect coastal communities around the world, including some of the most populous cities,

This photograph shows the Sizewell nuclear power station's close proximity to the sea in Suffolk, England.

such as New York, London, Singapore, and Tokyo. Scientists estimate that as much as half the world's population lives in coastal areas. Millions of people could be left homeless by storms and flooding. In addition, millions of acres of farmland could be made unusable because of the salt left behind by floodwater. This, in turn, could lead to widespread starvation.

The direct damage that rising seas cause to land and people is not the only problem. Around the world, nuclear power plants are frequently located on or near the coast because they need a constant supply of water to keep the reactor (the part of the facility where the fuel is processed) cool. For example, the United Kingdom's power plants at Hinkley Point and Sizewell are located only a few yards above sea level. Violent storms with high winds and huge waves could damage plants. If the damage is severe, the plants would be forced to shut down, resulting in the loss of electric power to thousands of people. If the power fails, the pumps would not be able to circulate water, and the reactor could overheat and explode.

Storms and rising seas could also flood waste dumps that are used to dispose of chemicals. The chemicals washed away from such dumps could contaminate nearby land and water supplies.

Historically, when climatic conditions changed, people migrated to areas with more favorable conditions. However, in the modern industrialized world, large populations are concentrated in coastal areas and cities, and there is no easy way for people to move to other areas to escape climatic changes.

SINKING ISLANDS

Some islands in the Maldives, a group of islands in the Indian Ocean near Sri Lanka, have been abandoned in recent years because rising seas have covered them. Worldwide, many tropical and subtropical islands are being battered by violent storms. Coral reefs, including Australia's Great Barrier Reef and many others in the Caribbean Sea, are being destroyed because of the rising temperatures of sea water. The destruction of these reefs, which help to protect the coastline, make coastal land even more vulnerable to the effects of rising seas and other climatic changes.

A house *(top)*, in Tuvalu, a western Pacific country made up of islands. The same house is flooded at high tide *(bottom)*. Tuvaluans fear that global warming is causing sea level changes that will make their country uninhabitable.

In the next decade, sea levels could rise 3 feet (about 1 m). This rise could have catastrophic effects on the people who live on Pacific islands, including the Maldives, Cocos, Tuvalu, Tokelau, Kiribati, Marshall, and Line islands. Global warming could increase both the level of the sea and the severity of tropical storms. Such storms could potentially devastate the populations of low-lying coastal regions. Typhoons could affect as many as 78 million people as swirling winds whip high seas into giant waves that crash over the coast. Those in southern Asia would be the hardest hit, but people would be affected worldwide. Because of tropical depressions and strong winds, the coast of China already faces high sea levels, and an additional rise could have terrible effects. The areas around the Black Sea, Thailand, and Indonesia are all extremely vulnerable.

The potential devastation is not limited to Pacific islands and Asian countries. Countries with river basins below sea level, such as Bangladesh and Egypt, will be affected as well. Coastal areas of the United States, such as those in Florida, the Gulf Coast, and California, are already at or below sea level. As water levels rise, these areas will become increasingly endangered.

THREATS TO AFRICAN NATIONS

Developing nations that lack the facilities to deal with massive flooding will be among the hardest hit by rising seas. Coastal communities such as those in the Gambia will be hammered by giant waves or huge storms. The Gambia is the smallest African nation, but it is densely populated. It has almost 185 miles (300 km) of shore along the Atlantic Ocean and the Gambia River. Fishing is the major source of income in the Gambia, but farming has been growing in importance. Much of the land along the shore has been cleared both to grow food for the increasing population and to grow flowers, which are sold as a cash crop to European markets. As a result, many of the mangrove trees have been cut down and no longer protect the shores, leaving the country even more vulnerable. As sea levels rise throughout the twenty-first century, the capital city of Bajul could find itself completely underwater. This would result in the destruction of homes, government and commercial buildings, and many historical sites. Erosion (washing away of soil) by the sea has already destroyed much coastal land. For example, the Gambia River contains James Island, where a British fort used during the slave-trading era (during the seventeenth and eighteenth centuries) is located. The island is located close to where the river meets the sea, and the river is therefore affected by the tide. The river has already washed away close to half the island. If seas continue to rise, this and other historical sites could be lost. However, protecting these sites and other important areas of the coast would cost more than the country can afford.

The Gambia is not alone in facing threats from rising seas. Other countries along the African coast are also in danger. According to a 2002 study titled "Perception and Reality: Assessing Priorities for Sustainable Development in the Niger Delta" by David Moffat and Olof Linde, 80 percent of Nigeria's coastline is in danger of being washed away by rising seas and the powerful waves of the Atlantic Ocean. Their conclusions are supported by a second study, "The Potential Effect of Global Warming and Sea Level Rise in Victoria Island and Lekki," by the Nigerian Institute for Ocean-ography and Marine Research. This report states that Victoria Island, off the coast of Nigeria, could lose up to 230 square miles (596 sq km) to rising seas. The loss of

Banding Together for Protection

The New Zealand National Institute of Water and Atmospheric Research has indicated that the climate of the Pacific Ocean's many island nations has changed over time. There is now more rainfall in the eastern and northern parts of the area, and it has become drier in the western and southern parts. This has caused frequent droughts on islands such as Fiji and New Caledonia. More threatening still is the fact that the sea in the region is rising about 0.13 inch (3.2 millimeters) per year.

Many island nations are developing countries. They do not have either the money or the technology to address potential disasters. The Alliance of Small Island States (AOSIS) was therefore created in 1990, at the Second World Climate Conference in Geneva, Switzerland. Its members include forty-three island countries from ocean regions throughout the world. The goal is to bring together the various small island nations whose survival is threatened by rising seas and other side effects of global warming. The organization works through the United Nations to address problems such as climate change. It also provides information on a variety of topics including energy and environmental issues.

coastal land in Nigeria could displace between 600,000 and 1.5 million people.

WHAT CAN WE DO?

The tools that scientists have at their disposal can be used to predict the likely effects of rising seas, but the future is in our hands. It is up to us to address the problems that are most likely causing this increase.

People's actions can take two forms: actions to protect land and people from the seas, and activities to reduce the production of greenhouse gases that cause global warming and affect sea levels.

PROTECTING THE COASTLINE

Efforts can be taken to limit—to some degree—the erosion, or wearing away, of the shoreline caused by higher seas. Such approaches include beach nourishment, which is the replenishment of the sand or soil that is washed away. Another approach, called hard stabilization, reinforces the coastline by erecting sea walls as barriers to block the sea. These methods, however, are very expensive. Beach nourishment can cost several million dollars per mile of coastline. This is beyond the means of the many developing countries that face the most danger. In addition, it is unlikely that barriers can be erected high enough along the endangered coasts to protect the land against massive tsunami-type waves, which can rise to over 20 feet (6 m).

STORMIER SKIES

Higher seas bring more frequent and stronger storms, such as hurricanes, cyclones (whirling windstorms), and

Proper sand replacement is one way to address sea erosion of coastlines. Above, in Spring Lake, New Jersey, researchers prepare the Coastal Research Amphibious Buggy (CRAB) for a trip into the Atlantic Ocean. CRAB is used in this beach replenishment project to plot the bottom of the ocean for the correct location of replacement sand.

typhoons. In areas likely to experience such storms, sea walls require reinforcement. In addition, it is necessary to engineer better drainage and runoff facilities to help reduce flood damage. It is also important to make buildings and facilities resistant to floods.

Realistic evacuation plans and routes need to be established for many coastal cities. The most vulnerable cities, however, are not accessible by road or do not have adequate facilities to care for large numbers of storm refugees. These are issues that will need to be addressed at both the local and national level.

NATURAL FORCES AND HUMAN ACTIONS

Global warming may not be the only cause of temperature increases that have led seas to rise. Earth's climate also changes naturally and goes through warmer and colder periods. However, given measurements that have been taken over the past decade, there is little doubt that the interaction of man-made and natural forces has led to an increase in temperature.

If we continue to produce greenhouse gases and engage in behaviors that contribute to global warming, the problem of rising seas will continue. We cannot control the natural forces that lead to changes in the climate, but we can control those that are man-made. The decisions we make affect the future not only of human beings but of all living things on Earth.

CONTROLLING THE MELTDOWN

People and governments around the world are concerned about the potentially disastrous effects of global warming, including the rising seas. In 1992, more than 150 governments signed the United Nations Framework Convention on Climate Change (UNFCCC).

The signers agreed to voluntarily reduce the levels of greenhouse gases that they produce. In 1997, the Kyoto Protocol updated the UNFCCC and made the voluntary reduction in greenhouse gases legally binding. The treaty was finally put into effect in February 2005, after years of delays. Its goal is to reduce the worldwide output of greenhouse gases by about 7 percent. The timeframe for achieving this goal is between 2008 and 2012.

However, some industrialized countries refused to sign the agreement. They were afraid that reducing emissions immediately would require making changes that would raise the cost of manufacturing products. The cost increase would then make their goods more expensive than those produced by developing nations. This could be bad for industrialized nations' economies.

In March 2001, President George W. Bush stated that the United States, the largest single producer of greenhouse gases, would not sign the agreement.

YOU CAN HELP

Gases that cause global warming come primarily from burning fossil fuels to make electricity and from automobile exhaust fumes. Individuals can help by buying energy-conserving appliances. They can also drive fuel-efficient cars. Hybrid cars, which are becoming more readily available, run on fuels other than gasoline and

In honor of the enactment of the Kyoto Protocol, a worldwide agreement that addresses global warming, Japanese lawmakers, above, are pictured with a huge handmade globe. After years of delays, the agreement went into effect on February 16, 2005. The arguments surrounding the protocol illustrate tradeoffs between what is best for economic prosperity and what is best for the planet and human survival.

therefore produce fewer greenhouse gases. People can also use public transportation or ride bicycles if they are going somewhere nearby. These things may not seem like they would make a huge difference, but if millions of people make these changes, it would lead to a reduction in the consumption of fossil fuels.

On a broader scale, people can write to their representatives in Congress and the president, urging them

Things You Can Do to Help

- Recycle bottles, cans, and paper.
- Buy food and toys that come in recyclable packaging, such as cardboard.
- Give away old toys to thrift shops, rummage sales, or charities. Passing them on to a new home reduces trash in landfills and therefore helps lessen the release of greenhouse gases.
- Turn off the lights, television, stereo, and other electronic devices when you're not using them.
- Use rechargeable batteries.
- When you or your family buy electronic devices such as computer monitors, look for those with the Energy Star symbol, which means that they use less electricity.
- Join organizations, such as the Sierra Club (www.sierraclub.org), that work to protect the natural environment.

to support international proposals to reduce industrial emissions. People and governments around the world must work together to address the problems of global warming and rising seas, which affect all living things on Earth.

atom A basic particle of matter.

beach nourishment The addition of sand or soil to the coast to protect it from being eroded by the sea.

cash crop A crop grown and sold for money rather than consumed locally.

cyclone A violent whirling windstorm.

depression In weather, an area of low pressure surrounded by areas of higher atmospheric pressure.

ecologist A scientist who studies the environment.

ecosystem The plants and animals that live in a certain environment.

erosion The loss of land from forces such as water and wind.

fossil fuels Materials used for fuel, such as oil, coal, or natural gas, that formed in the earth from plant or animal remains.

generator A machine that converts one form of energy, such as kerosene, into another form of energy, such as electricity.

glacier A large sheet of slowly moving ice.

global warming An increase in the average temperature of the atmosphere.

greenhouse effect The process in which molecules of gases in the atmosphere absorb sunlight and reflect it back to the earth, thus warming Earth's surface.

greenhouse gases Gases, such as carbon dioxide and nitrous oxide, that contribute to global warming.

ice age An extended period of time during which there is a decrease in the average temperature of the earth's climate and glaciers cover a large part of the planet.

laser altimetry A method of measuring the heights of surfaces by measuring the time it takes for them to reflect back light from a laser.

microwave A short electromagnetic wave that can be used in radar, radio transmissions, and in cooking and heating devices.

molecule A group of atoms bound together.

parasite An organism that lives in, benefits from, and harms another living thing.

passive microwave imaging The use of satellite-based sensors to map objects on Earth by the microwave energy they give off.

photosynthesis The process by which plants use carbon dioxide, water, and sunlight to produce food.

sea level The average level of the sea halfway between high tide and low tide.

sensor A device that detects energy, such as light or heat, given off by an object.

storm surge A sudden increase in the height of the sea due to a hurricane.

tsunami A gigantic ocean wave.

typhoon A violent tropical storm with high winds.

FOR MORE INFORMATION

Environment Canada
70 Crémazie Street
Gatineau, QC K1A 0H3
Canada
(800) 668-6767 or (819) 997-2800
Web site: http://www.ec.gc.ca

Greenpeace
702 H Street NW
Washington, DC 20001
(202) 462-1177
Web site: http://www.greenpeace.org

National Snow and Ice Data Center (NSIDC)
449 UCB
University of Colorado
Boulder, CO 80309-0449
(303) 492-6199
Web site: http://www.NSIDC.org

Sierra Club
National Headquarters
85 Second Street, 2nd Floor
San Francisco, CA 94105
(415) 977-5500
Web site: http://www.sierraclub.org

WEB SITES

Due to the changing nature of Internet links, the Rosen Publishing Group, Inc., has developed an online list of Web sites related to the subject of this book. This site is updated regularly. Please use this link to access the list:

http://www.rosenlinks.com/eet/thrs

FOR FURTHER READING

EarthWorks Group. *50 Simple Things Kids Can Do to Save the Earth*. New York, NY: Andrews & McMeel, 1990.

Friedman, Katherine. *What If the Polar Ice Caps Melted?* Danbury, CT: Children's Press, 2002.

Parks, Peggy. *Global Warming*. San Diego, CA: Lucent Books, 2003.

Pringle, Laurence. *Global Warming: The Threat of Earth's Changing Climate*. New York, NY: Seastar Books, 2001.

Taylor, Barbara. *How to Save the Planet*. Danbury, CT: Franklin Watts, 2001.

Weller, Dave, and Mick Hart. *Arctic & Antarctic*. San Diego, CA: Silver Dolphin, 1996.

BIBLIOGRAPHY

Arendt, Anthony A., Keith A. Echelmeyer, William D. Harrison, Craig S. Lingle, and Virginia B. Valentine. "Rapid Wastage of Alaska Glaciers and Their Contribution to Rising Sea Level." *Science*, Vol. 297, No. 5580, July 19, 2002.

Atterton, Gary. "Will the Gambia Go Under?" *Wide World*, Vol. 12, No. 14, April 2001.

Dennison, Derek. "Icy Indicators of Global Warming." *World Watch*, January/February 1993.

Dunn, Seth. "Antarctic Ice Shelves See Another Big Breakup." *World Watch*, Vol. 12, No. 1, January/ February 1999.

EPA. "Global Warming: Impacts; South Florida." Retrieved June 12, 2005 (http://yosemite.epa.gov/ oar/globalwarming.nsf/o/85256c870070ee7285256 c31005ddd4f?OpenDocument).

Financial Times Information. "Rising Seas Threat to Islands' Ancient Sites." *Europe Intelligence Wire*, August 16, 2004.

Foley, Grover. "The Threat of Rising Seas." *Ecologist*, Vol. 29, No. 2, March/April, 1999.

Goldberg, Jeff. "Water World?" *Science World*, Vol. 52, No. 5, November 3, 1995.

Gornitz, Vivian. "Rising Seas: A View from New York City." Goddard Institute for Space Studies. Retrieved

June 12, 2005 (http://www.giss.nasa.gov/research/briefs/gornitz_05).

Government of Canada. "Regional Impacts: Nova Scotia." Retrieved June 12, 2005 (http://www.climatechange.gc.ca/english/affect/prov_territory/ns.asp).

Moore, Curtis. "Awash in a Rising Sea." *International Wildlife*, January/February 2002.

Nash, Madeleine. "Where the Waters Are Rising: A Close-up Look at the Low-Lying Maldives, Where Global Warming Hits the Seawall." *Time*, Vol. 165, No. 17, April 25, 2005.

National Research Council. *Studies in Geophysics: Sea-Level Change*. National Academy Press, Washington, DC: 1990.

National Snow and Ice Data Center. "State of the Cryosphere." Retrieved August 12, 2005 (http://nsidc.org/sotc).

Ocean Conserve. "Look at Past Sea-level Rise Points to Troubling Future." Retrieved June 12, 2005. (http://www.oceanconserve.info/articles/read.asp?linkid=36197).

O'Meara, Molly. "Antarctic Ice Shelf Crumbling." *World Watch*, Vol. 1, No. 4, July/August 1998.

Pilkey, Orrin H., and J. Andrew G. Cooper. "Society and Sea Level Rise." *Science*, Vol. 303, No. 5665, March 19, 2004.

Raufu, Abiodun, "Africa Underwater: Nigeria's Coastline is Besieged by Global Warming." *E*, Vol. 13, No. 2, March/April 2002.

"Saxby's Prediction." *Hawke's Bay Herald*, October 12, 1869. Retrieved June 22, 2005 (http://www.magma.ca/~jdreid/hawke.htm).

Schwartz, Pete, and Doug Randall. "An Abrupt Climate Change Scenario and Its Implications for United States National Security." U.S. Pentagon, October 2003. Retrieved June 12, 2005 (http://www.ldeo.columbia.edu/edu/dees/V1003/readings/Pentagon.pdf).

United Press International. "Society Faces Collision with Rising Seas." *UPI Perspectives*, June 24, 2004.

INDEX

ABOUT THE AUTHOR

Ellen Foxxe has a BA from Harvard University and extensive experience working at companies that perform environmental testing services and provide environmental testing equipment. She divides her time between New Orleans and Boston.

PHOTO CREDITS

Cover © Rafiqur Rahman/Reuters/Corbis; pp. 1, 8, 13, 21, 41, 51 © AP/Wide World Photos; pp. 4–5 © Peter Essick/ Aurora Photo; p. 7 © Lt. Eric Baum/Miami-Dade Fire Rescue/ Handout/Reuters/Corbis; p. 10 © Smiley N. Pool/Dallas Morning News/Corbis; p. 12 © David R. Frazier/Photo Researchers, Inc.; p. 15 © Getty Images, Inc.; p. 17 © Roger Braithwaite/Peter Arnold, Inc.; p. 22 © Doug Wilson/Corbis; p. 24 © Ashley Cooper/Picimpact/Corbis; p. 26 © Publiphoto/ Photo Researchers, Inc.; p. 27 by Thomas Forget; p. 29 © Rickey Rogers/Reuters/Corbis; p. 30 © Sime/Corbis; p. 31 © Baerbel K. Luccitta/U.S. Geological Survey/Photo Researchers, Inc.; p. 34 © NASA/Goddard Space Flight Center Scientific Visualization Studio; p. 35 © U.S. Navy; p. 36 © NASA/ Goddard Space Flight Center; p. 38 © NOAA; p. 40 © Reuters/Corbis; p. 44 © Skyscan/Science Photo Library; p. 46 © Torsten Blackwood/AFP/Getty Images, Inc.; p. 54 © Issei Kato/Reuters/Corbis.

Designer: Thomas Forget; Editor: Liz Gavril
Photo Researcher: Hillary Arnold